UPDATED EDITION

Guess What!

Student's Book 1
with eBook

American English

Susannah Reed with Kay Bentley

Series Editor: Lesley Koustaff

CAMBRIDGE

Contents

			Page
Hello!			**4**
Vocabulary	blue, green, orange, pink, purple, red, yellow		6–7
Grammar	Hello, I'm … , What's your name?, Goodbye. ● How old are you? I'm … ● Numbers 1–10 ● What's your favorite color? My favorite color's …		8–9
Story value	Be curious		10
Talk time	*Look! It's a lizard!*		11
Animal sounds	*p* ● A pink and purple panda.		
CLIL: Art	What color is it?		12–13

1 **School**			**14**
Vocabulary	board, book, chair, desk, door, eraser, pen, pencil, pencil case, window		16–17
Grammar	How many (chairs) can you see? ● Stand up, please.		18–19
Story value	Make friends		20
Talk time	*Hello. My name's Ravi.*		21
Animal sounds	*b* ● A bear with a blue book.		
CLIL: Science	What material is it?		22–23

2 **Toys**			**24**
Vocabulary	art set, ball, bike, camera, computer, computer game, doll, kite, robot, teddy bear		26–27
Grammar	What's this? ● Is it a (ball)?		28–29
Story value	Say thank you		30
Talk time	*Happy birthday!*		31
Animal sounds	*t* ● A turtle with two teddy bears.		
CLIL: Science	Is it electric?		32–33
Review	Units I–2		34–35

3 **Family**			**36**
Vocabulary	aunt, brother, cousin, dad, grandma, grandpa, mom, sister, uncle		38–39
Grammar	Who's this? ● Who's that?		40–41
Story value	Love your family		42
Talk time	*Hello, Grandma. How are you?*		43
Animal sounds	*d* ● A dolphin in a red desk.		
CLIL: Geography	What continent is it?		44–45

4 **At home**			**46**
Vocabulary	apartment, balcony, bathroom, bedroom, dining room, hallway, house, kitchen, living room, yard		48–49
Grammar	Where are you? / I'm in (the kitchen). ● Where's (the doll)?		50–51
Story value	Take care of things		52
Talk time	*Take care of things!*		53
Animal sounds	*a* ● An ant with an apple.		
CLIL: Math	What shape is it?		54–55
Review	Units 3–4		56–57

		Page
5 My body		**58**
Vocabulary	arms, ears, eyes, feet, hair, hands, head, legs, mouth, nose	60–61
Grammar	I have (a red head and green eyes). ● Do you have (a yellow nose)?	62–63
Story value	Be clean	64
Talk time	*Wash your feet, please.*	65
Animal sounds	*i* ● An iguana with pink ink.	
CLIL: Science	What sense is it?	66–67
6 Food		**68**
Vocabulary	apple, banana, bread, cheese, chicken, egg, juice, milk, orange, water	70–71
Grammar	I like (bananas). ● Do you like (eggs)?	72–73
Story value	Be patient	74
Talk time	*Can I have four apples, please?*	75
Animal sounds	*e* ● An elephant with ten eggs.	
CLIL: Science	Where is food from?	76–77
Review	Units 5–6	78–79
7 Actions		**80**
Vocabulary	climb, dance, draw, jump, paint, play soccer, ride a bike, run, sing, swim	82–83
Grammar	I can (swim)! ● Can you (ride a bike)?	84–85
Story value	Help your friends	86
Talk time	*You can do it!*	87
Animal sounds	*u* ● An umbrella bird can jump.	
CLIL: Math	What's the number?	88–89
8 Animals		**90**
Vocabulary	bird, crocodile, elephant, giraffe, hippo, lion, monkey, snake, spider, zebra	92–93
Grammar	(Elephants) are (big). ● (Elephants) have (long trunks).	94–95
Story value	Respect animals	96
Talk time	*It's small. Respect animals.*	97
Animal sounds	*o* ● An octopus in an orange box.	
CLIL: Science	How do animals move?	98–99
Review	Units 7–8	100–101
My sounds		102–103

3

Hello!

Guess What!

5

1 🎧 0.01 Listen. Who's speaking?

2 🎧 0.02 Listen, point, and say.

3 🎧 0.03 Listen and find.

Find Leo

4 Say the chant.

5 Think Look and say the name.

Number 1. David.

1

3

2

4

6 🎧 0.07 **Listen, look, and say.**

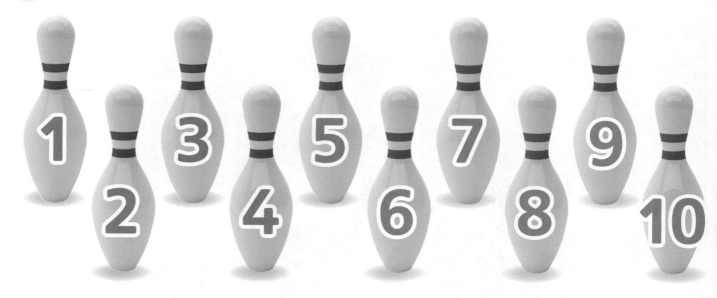

7 **Look and match.**

8 🎧 0.08 **Now listen and check.**

Grammar: *Numbers 1–10*

→ Workbook page 6

9  **0.10 Listen, point, and say.**

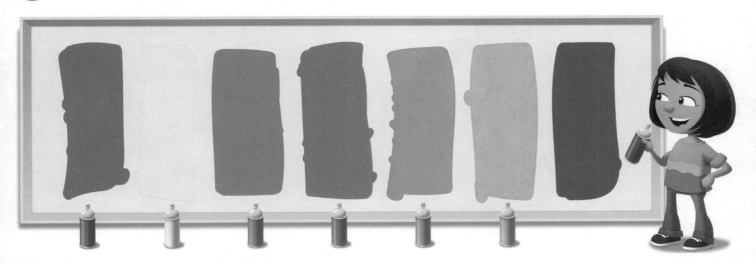

10 0.11 Sing the song.

11 About Me **Ask and answer.**

How old are you?   I'm six.

What's your favorite color?   My favorite color's blue.

Grammar: *My favorite color's …*

12 🎧 0.13 ▶ Story Listen and watch.

10 Value: Be curious

→ Workbook page 8

13   Listen and act.

Animal sounds

14  Listen and say.

A **p**ink and **p**urple **p**anda.

What color is it?

1 🎧 0.18 Listen and say.

2 CLIL ▶ Watch the video.

3 Say the color.

Number 1. Orange.   Yes.

Guess What!

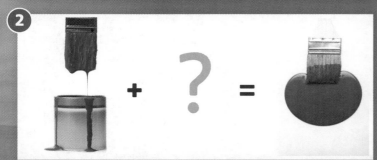

Let's collaborate!

OUR COLOR COLLAGE

think   find
choose   compare
color
create

1 School

Look!

Guess What!

15

1 🎧 1.01 Listen. Who's speaking?

2 🎧 1.02 Listen, point, and say.

3 🎧 1.03 Listen and find.

4 🎧 1.05 Say the chant.

5 Think Look and find five differences.

Picture 1. A purple pen.   Picture 2. A purple pencil.

6 (1.07) Sing the song.

7 (1.08) Listen and answer the questions.

How many chairs can you see?

Six!

1 2 3 4 5

Grammar fun!

Grammar: *How many chairs can you see?*

→ Workbook page 14

8 🎧 (1.09) **Listen, point, and say.**

9 🎧 (1.10) **Listen and do the action.**

10 **Play the game.**

Open your book.

Grammar: *Stand up, please.* *Grammar fun!* ▶

20 Value: Make friends

→ Workbook page 16

12   **Listen and act.**

Animal sounds

13 🎧 **Listen and say.**

A **bear** with a **blue book.**

What material is it?

1 🎧 1.17 Listen and say.

 **1**
 **2**
 **3**
 **4**

2 CLIL ▶ Watch the video.

3 Look and say *wood, plastic, metal,* or *glass.*

Number 1. Wood.   Yes.

Guess What!

Let's collaborate!

 **1**
 **2**
 **3**
 **4**

OUR MATERIALS POSTER

plastic

create

draw

wood   metal   glass

② Toys

Look!

Guess What! theme

25

1 (2.01) Listen. Who's speaking?

2 (2.02) Listen, point, and say.

3 (2.03) Listen and find.

Find Leo

→ Workbook page 20

Say the chant.

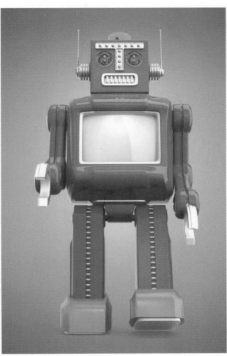

5 (Think) **Look and find five missing toys in picture 2.**

The yellow ball.

Vocabulary **27**

6 🎧 2.07 **Listen, look, and say.**

7 Think **Look and say.** What's this? It's a kite.

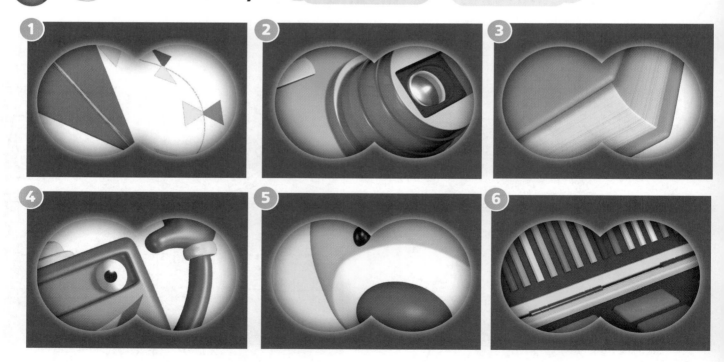

8 🎧 2.08 **Now listen and check.**

  Grammar: *What's this?* → Workbook page 22

9 🎧 2.10 **Sing the song.**

10 Play the game.

Is it a ball?

No, it isn't.

Grammar: *Is it a ball?*   Grammar fun!   **29**

2.13 **Story** **Listen and watch.**

Value: Say thank you

→ Workbook page 24

12 **Talk Time** **Listen and act.**

Animal sounds

13 (2.16) **Listen and say.**

A **t**urtle with **t**wo **t**eddy bears.

Is it electric?

1

2

3

2 CLIL ▶ Watch the video.

3 Look and say *it's electric* or *it isn't electric.*

Number 1. It isn't electric.   Yes.

Guess What!

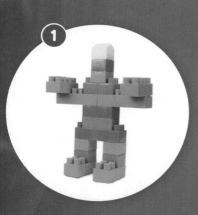

1

2

3

4

Let's collaborate!

OUR BOARD GAME

count

play   colors

1 3 5 7 9
2 4 6 8 0
numbers

questions ??

toys

Review Units 1 and 2

1 Look and say the word.

Number 1. Desk.

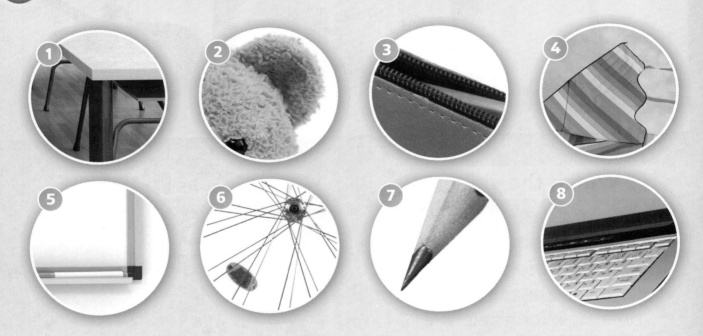

2 🎧 2.20 Listen and say the color.

34

→ Workbook pages 28–29

3 Play the game.

Blue
What's this?
It's a (pencil case).

Red
Is it a (teddy bear)?
Yes, it is.
Is it an (art set)?
No, it isn't.

Finish

Yellow
How many books can you see?
I can see (six books).

12

11

10

9

8

6

5

7

4

3

2

1

Start

3 Family

Look!

Guess What!

1  (3.01) **Listen. Who's speaking?**

2 (3.02) **Listen, point, and say.**

① grandma ② grandpa

③ dad ④ mom ⑤ uncle ⑥ aunt

⑦ brother ⑧ sister ⑨ cousin

3 (3.03) **Listen and find.**

Find Leo

4 🎧 3.04 **Say the chant.**

5 🎧 3.05 (Think) **Listen and say *yes* or *no*.** This is my dad. No!

6 (3.07) **Sing the song.**

7 (3.08) (Think) **Listen and say *yes* or *no*.**

1   2   3   4

Grammar fun! ▶

40   Grammar: *Who's this?*   → Workbook page 32

8 3.09 **Listen, look, and say.**

1

2

9 3.10 **Listen and say the color.**

10 About Me **Draw your family. Ask and answer.**

Who's this?   It's my brother. His name's Freddy.

Who's that? Is that your sister?   No, it isn't. It's my cousin.

→ Workbook page 33   Grammar: *Who's that?*

Grammar fun!

41

12 🎧 3.14 Talk Time Listen and act.

Animal sounds

13 🎧 3.15 Listen and say.

A **d**olphin in a re**d** **d**esk.

What continent is it?

Ottawa

Madrid

Tokyo

Lima

1 🎧 3.17 Listen and say.

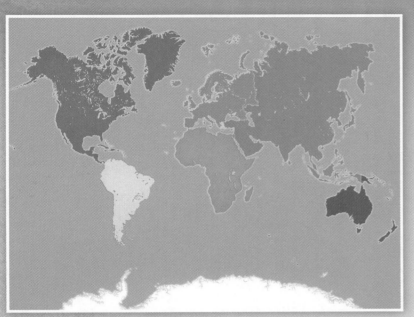

1 North America
2 South America
3 Europe
4 Africa
5 Asia
6 Australia
7 Antarctica

Guess What!

2 CLIL ▶ Watch the video.

3 What continent are they from?

My name's Akiko. I'm from Tokyo.

My name's Zack. I'm from Ottawa.

My name's Luiz. I'm from Lima.

My name's Sofia. I'm from Madrid.

Let's collaborate!

family   look   discuss

OUR CHILDREN OF THE WORLD BOOKLET

agree   research   continent

→ Workbook page 36   CLIL: Geography   45

4 At home

Look!

Guess What! theme

1 🎧 4.01 **Listen. Who's speaking?**

2 🎧 4.02 **Listen, point, and say.**

① house

② bathroom

③ bedroom

④ apartment

⑤ dining room

⑥ living room

⑦ balcony

⑧ kitchen

⑨ hallway

⑩ yard

Find Leo

3 🎧 4.03 **Listen and find.**

4 🎧 4.04 Say the chant.

5 Think Look and say the room.

Number 1. Dining room.

6 🎧 4.06 Listen, look, and say.

1

2

3

7 🎧 4.07 Listen and say Apartment 1 or Apartment 2.

Where's your mom?   Apartment 2.

She's in the bedroom.

Apartment 1

Apartment 2

Grammar fun!

Grammar: *Where are you? / I'm in the kitchen.*   → Workbook page 40

8 (4.08) **Sing the song.**

9 (4.09) **Listen and say _yes_ or _no_.**

10 **Ask and answer.**

Where's the doll?

Yes!

It's under the table.

Grammar: _Where's the doll?_

Grammar fun!

12   **Listen and act.**

Animal sounds

13 🎧 4.14 **Listen and say.**

An ant with an apple.

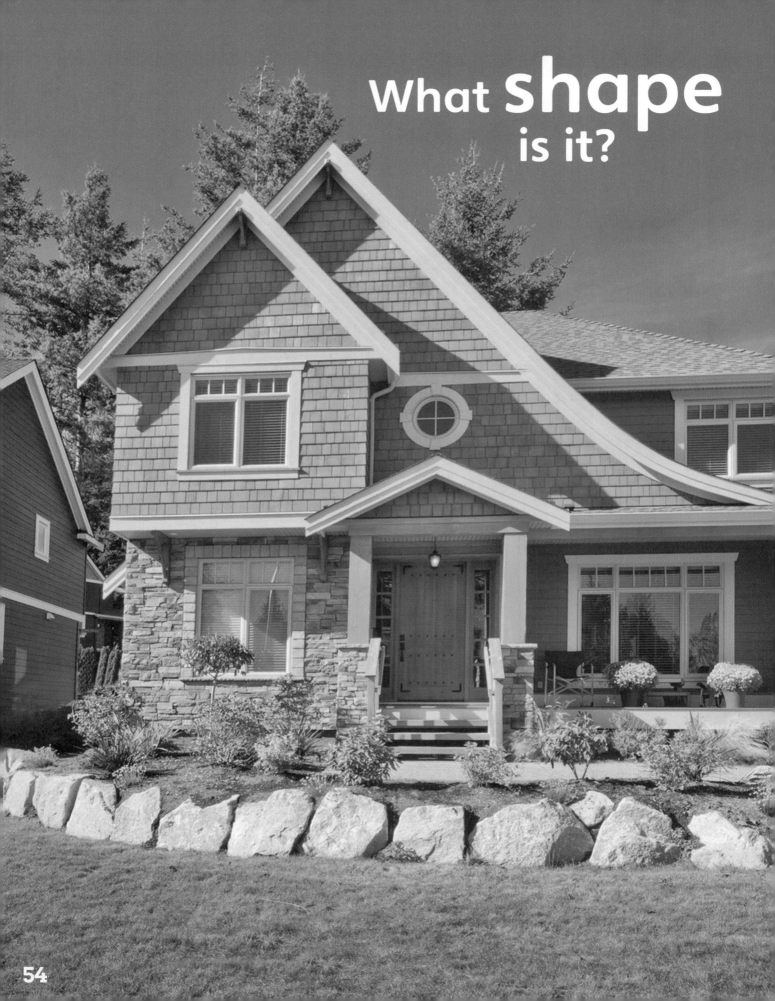

What shape is it?

1 🎧 4.16 Listen and say.

1

circle

2

triangle

3

square

2 ▶ CLIL Watch the video.

3 Look and say *circle*, *triangle*, or *square*.

What's this?   It's a circle!

1

2

3

4

Guess What?

Let's collaborate!

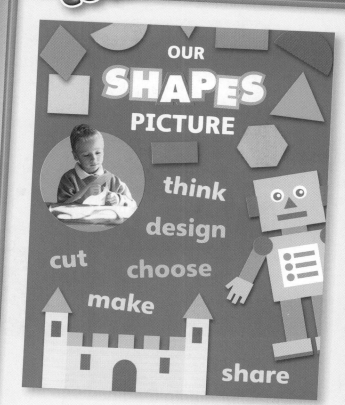

OUR SHAPES PICTURE

think
design
cut
choose
make
share

Review Units 3 and 4

1 Look and say the words.

Number 1. Yard.

2 (4.17) Listen and say the color.

→ Workbook pages 46–47

3 Play the game.

Yellow
Where's the (computer)?
It's (in) the (bedroom).

Orange
Where's your (grandma)?
(She) is in the (bedroom).

5

6

7

8

4

9

3

10

2

1

11

Start

Finish

57

5 My body

Look!

Guess What!

59

1 🎧 5.01 Listen. Who's speaking?

2 🎧 5.02 Listen, point, and say.

1 head
2 nose
3 eyes
4 hair
5 ears
6 arms
7 mout
8 hands
9 feet
10 legs

BIKE CLUB

3 🎧 5.03 Listen and find.

Find Leo

4 **Say the chant.**

5 (Think) **Look and say the action.** Number 1. Stamp your feet.

1

2

3

6 🎧 5.06 **Listen, look, and say.**

7 🎧 5.07 Think **Listen and say the name.**

i-Lin   i-Tex   i-Zak   i-Con

Grammar fun! ▶   Grammar: *I have a red head and green eyes.*   → Workbook page 50

8 🎧 5.09 Sing the song.

9 Ask and answer.

→ Workbook page 51   Grammar: *Do you have a yellow nose?*   Grammar fun!   **63**

10 🎧 5.10 ▶ Story Listen and watch.

64   Value: Be clean

→ Workbook page 52

11   5.12 **Listen and act.**

Animal sounds

12 5.13 **Listen and say.**

An iguana with pink ink.

What **sense** is it?

1 🎧 5.15 Listen and say.

sight

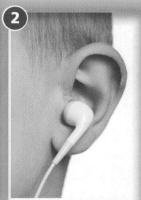
hearing

smell

taste

touch

2 CLIL ▶ Watch the video.

3 Look and say the senses.

Number 1. Sight and touch.   Yes.

Guess What!

Let's collaborate!

OUR **EXERCISE VIDEO**

choose
listen and do
say
move
think   film

6 Food

Look!

Guess What! theme

69

1 (6.01) **Listen. Who's speaking?**

2 (6.02) **Listen, point, and say.**

1 chicken

2 water

3 orange

4 cheese

5 milk

6 egg

7 apple

8 banana

9 juice

10 bread

3 (6.03) **Listen and find.**

Find Leo

Say the chant.

5 (Think) **Look and find five differences.**

Picture 1. I have chicken.

Picture 2. I have cheese.

6 🎧 6.06 **Listen, look, and say.**

7 🎧 6.07 (Think) **Listen and say the name.**

I like chicken and I like bananas …   Kim.

Alex	✗	✓	✗	✓
Sasha	✓	✗	✓	✗
Sam	✗	✓	✓	✗
Kim	✓	✓	✓	✗

Grammar fun! ▶

Grammar: *I like bananas.*   → Workbook page 58

8 🎧 6.09 **Sing the song.**

9 (About Me) **Play the game.**

Number 1. Yellow. Do you like chicken with apples?   No, I don't.

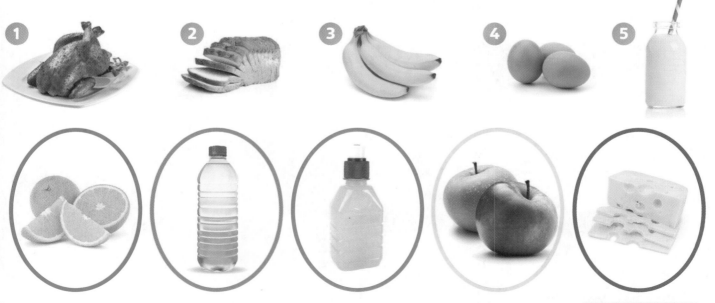

→ Workbook page 59   Grammar: *Do you like eggs?*   **Grammar fun!** ▶

11   Talk Time Listen and act.

Animal sounds

12 Listen and say.

**An elephant
with ten eggs.**

Where is **food** from?

1 🎧 6.15 Listen and say.

plants

1

2

3

animals

4

5

6

2 CLIL ▶ Watch the video.

3 Look and say *plant* or *animal*.

Number 1. Plant.   Yes!

1

2

3

4

Guess What!

Let's collaborate!

OUR FOOD SURVEY

like

plants

animals

✓ ✗

ask and answer

?

count

compare

→ Workbook page 62   CLIL: Science   **77**

Review Units 5 and 6

1 Look and say the word.

Number 1. Mouth.

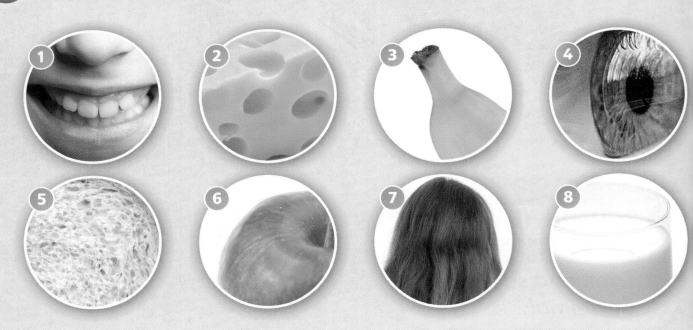

2 (6.16) Listen and say the name.

Tony

Ana

Lily

Ravi

→ Workbook pages 64–65

3 Play the game.

Finish

Start

Blue
I don't have (four hands).
I have a (nose).

Green
I like / I don't like
(bananas).

Look!

Guess What!

81

1 🎧 7.01 **Listen. Who's speaking?**

2 🎧 7.02 **Listen, point, and say.**

Come to a **Festival** at the park!

① run
② jump
③ swim
④ climb
⑤ play soccer
⑥ ride a bike
⑦ draw
⑧ paint
⑨ dance
⑩ sing

3 🎧 7.03 **Listen and find.**

Find Leo

4 🎧 7.04 Say the chant.

5 Look and match. Then say the action.

> Number 1. Green.
> Play soccer.

1  **2**  **3**  **4**

→ Workbook page 67

Vocabulary **83**

6 🎧 7.06 **Listen, look, and say.**

1

2

7 🎧 7.07 **Listen and say the number.** I can run. Six

1

2

3

4

5

6

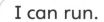

Grammar fun! ▶

Grammar: *I can swim!*

→ Workbook page 68

8 🎧 7.09 Sing the song.

9 About Me Ask and answer.

Can you ride a bike?

Yes, I can.

Grammar: *Can you ride a bike?*   Grammar fun!

11 🎧 7.12 (Talk Time) **Listen and act.**

Animal sounds

12 🎧 7.13 **Listen and say.**

An **umbrella** bird can j**u**mp.

What's the number?

1 7.15 **Listen and say.**

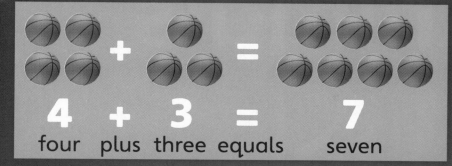

4 + 3 = 7

four   plus   three   equals   seven

8   − 2 =   6

eight   minus two equals   six

Guess What!

2 CLIL **Watch the video.**

3 **Find the number. Then say the words.**

Five balls plus five balls equals ten balls.

Yes!

Let's collaborate!

①  + = ?

② − = ?

③ − ? =

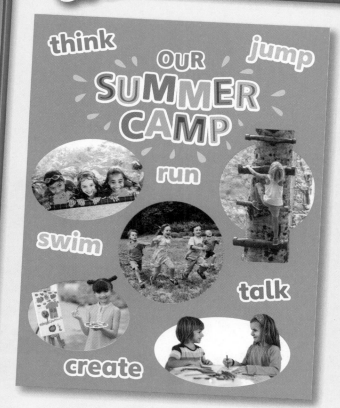

think   jump

OUR SUMMER CAMP

run

swim

talk

create

8 Animals

Look!

Guess What!

1 🎧 8.01 **Listen. Who's speaking?**

2 🎧 8.02 **Listen, point, and say.**

1 giraffe
2 monkey
3 elephant
4 bird
5 snake
6 hippo
7 zebra
8 lion
9 spider
10 crocodile

Africa

Find Leo

3 🎧 8.03 **Listen and find.**

4 🎧 8.04 Say the chant.

5 Think Look and say the animal.

Number 1. A snake.

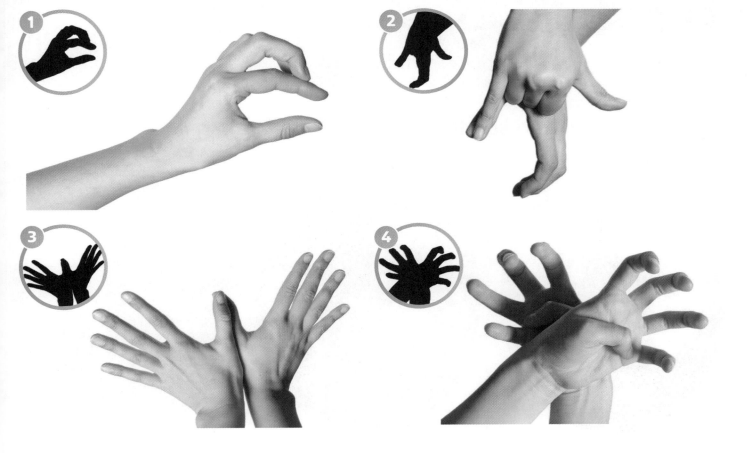

6 (8.06) **Listen, point, and say.**

long   short

big   small

tall   short

7 (8.07) **Listen and say the number.**

1

2

3

Grammar fun!

Grammar: *Elephants are big.*   → Workbook page 76

8 (8.08) **Sing the song.**

9 (8.09) **Listen and say *yes* or *no*.**

10 **Look and find five mistakes.**

Giraffes don't have short necks.
Giraffes have long necks.

→ Workbook page 77   Grammar: *Elephants have long trunks.*

Grammar fun!

ZOO

Value: **Respect animals**

→ Workbook page 78

12   **Listen and act.**

Animal sounds

13   **Listen and say.**

An octopus in an orange box.

How do animals move?

1 🎧 8.15 Listen and say.

1 walk

2 fly

3 slither

2 CLIL ▶ Watch the video.

3 Look and say *walk*, *fly*, or *slither*.

A spider can walk.   Yes.

Guess What!

1

2

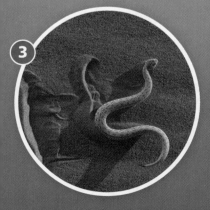

3

4

Let's collaborate!

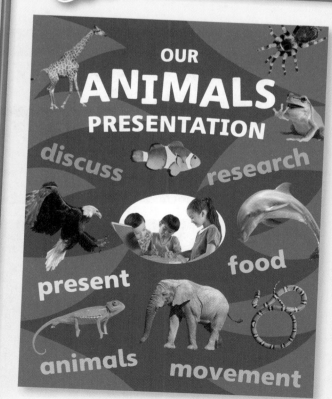

OUR ANIMALS PRESENTATION

discuss   research

present   food

animals   movement

→ Workbook page 80   CLIL: Science   99

Review Units 7 and 8

1 Look and say the words.

> Number 1.
> Play soccer.

2 🎧 8.16 Listen and say the number.

→ Workbook pages 82–83

3 **Play the game.**

Orange
I can (play soccer).

Green
(Giraffes) have (long necks).

Red
(Birds) are (small).

My sounds

panda

bear

turtle

dolphin

ant

iguana

elephant

umbrella bird

octopus

Acknowledgments

Many thanks to everyone in the excellent team at Cambridge University Press & Assessment in Spain, the UK, and India.

The authors and publishers would like to thank the following contributors:
Blooberry Design: concept design, cover design, book design
Hyphen: publishing management, page make-up
Ann Thomson: art direction
Gareth Boden: commissioned photography
Jon Barlow: commissioned photography
Ian Harker: class audio recording
John Marshall Media: "Grammar fun" recordings
Robert Lee, Dib Dib Dub Studios: song and chant composition
Vince Cross: theme tune composition
James Richardson: arrangement of theme tune
Phaebus: "CLIL" video production
Kiki Foster: "Look!" video production
Bill Smith Group: "Grammar fun" and story animations
Sounds Like Mike Ltd: "Grammar Fun" video production

The authors and publishers acknowledge the following sources of copyright material and are grateful for the permissions granted. While every effort has been made, it has not always been possible to identify the sources of all the material used, or to trace all copyright holders. If any omissions are brought to our notice, we will be happy to include the appropriate acknowledgements on reprinting and in the next update to the digital edition, as applicable.

Key: U = Unit.

Photography

The following photos are sourced from Getty Images:
U0: Fertnig/iStock/Getty Images Plus; szefei/iStock/Getty Images Plus; Mike Kemp/Tetra images; plusphoto/iStock/Getty Images Plus; matty2x4/E+; skodonnell/E+; crossbrain66/E+; cscredon/E+; Weekend Images Inc./E+; BirdImages/E+; PhotoTalk/E+; Apassara Kanha/EyeEm; **U1:** kali9/E+; UltraONEs/iStock/Getty Images Plus; Kimberly Hosey/Moment; MiguelMalo/iStock/Getty Images Plus; Dimitris66/iStock/Getty Images Plus; szefei/iStock/Getty Images Plus; jskiba/E+; hayatikayhan/iStock/Getty Images Plus; Ng Sok Lian/EyeEm; Lucy Lambriex/DigitalVision; Bojan Vlahovic/E+; Natthawut Punyosaeng/EyeEm; Prasert Krainukul/Moment; mirjanajovic/DigitalVision Vectors; SolStock/E+; **U2:** gio_banfi/DigitalVision Vectors; Kutay Tanir/Photodisc; Jupiterimages/Stockbyte; Isabel Pavia/Moment; **U3:** Rick Gomez/Tetra images; Ariel Skelley/DigitalVision; Stockbyte; ViewStock; Tanong Abhivadanasiri/EyeEm; Tetra Images; Floortje/E+; **U4:** Vaughn Greg/Getty Images; Simon Montgomery/Getty Images; Compassionate Eye Foundation/Rob Daly/OJO Images Ltd/DigitalVision; Taiyou Nomachi/DigitalVision; chuckcollier/E+; aliaksei_putau/iStock/Getty Images Plus; Mel Yates/DigitalVision; **U5:** annie-claude/iStock/Getty Images Plus; szefei/iStock/Getty Images Plus; ArtMarie/E+; acilo/iStock/Getty Images Plus; BJI/Blue Jean Images; Robert Daly/OJO Images; MesquitaFMS/E+; Tom Merton/OJO Images; Lucas Ninno/Moment; **U6:** Jack Hollingsworth/Getty Images; Jose Luis Pelaez Inc/DigitalVision; Wavebreakmedia Ltd/Wavebreak Media/Getty Images Plus; saiko3p/iStock/Getty Images Plus; aliaksei_putau/iStock/Getty Images Plus; Yevgen Romanenko/Moment; Richard Sharrocks/Moment; lacaosa/Moment; milanfoto/E+; happyfoto/E+; antonios mitsopoulos/Moment Open; Jose Luis Pelaez Inc/DigitalVision; stockcam/E+; **U7:** szefei/iStock/Getty Images Plus; buydeepphoto/iStock/Getty Images Plus; FatCamera/E+; Paul Biris/Moment; Thomas Barwick/Stone; wera Rodsawang/Moment; skynesher/E+; **U8:** Stuart Westmorland/Corbis Documentary; Elizabeth W. Kearley/Moment; A.Töfke Cologne Germay/Moment; Lintao Zhang/Staff/Getty Images News; Adria Photography/Moment; Istvan Kadar Photography/Moment; Mark Miller Photos/Photodisc; Surasak Suwanmake/Moment; Yannick Tylle/Corbis Documentary; Antagain/E+; Martin Harvey/The Image Bank; BirdImages/E+; blue jean images; Mike Hill/Stone; Life On White/Photodisc; Petr Pikora/EyeEm; stilllifephotographer/Stone; Sally Anscombe/Moment; DENIS-HUOT/hemis.fr; Ableimages/Photodisc; Picture by Tambako the Jaguar/Moment Open; David Muir/Stone; Aldo Pavan/The Image Bank; GEN UMEKITA/Moment; Larry Keller, Lititz Pa./Moment; Picture by Tambako the Jaguar/Moment; Dethan Punalur/Stockbyte; paulafrench/iStock/Getty Images Plus.

The following photos are sourced from other libraries:
U0: Pat Canova/Alamy; Margot Hartford/Alamy; Jose Luis Pelaez Inc/Tetra Images, LLC/Alamy; Leigh Prather/Shutterstock; Jaechang Yoo/TongRo Images/Alamy; Valery Voennyy/Alamy; **U1:** Joshua Davenport/Shutterstock; pics five/Shutterstock; City Living/Alamy; My Life Graphic/Shutterstock; Vorobyeva/Shutterstock; Jesus Keller/Shutterstock; Foonia/Shutterstock; ETIENjones/Shutterstock; sirtravelalot/Shutterstock; **U2:** stable/Shutterstock; Chesky/Shutterstock; Fabrice Lerouge/ONOKY - Photononstop/Alamy; Jolanta Wojcicka/Shutterstock; Andriy Rabchun/Shutterstock; ffolas/Shutterstock; prapann/Shutterstock; mekcar/Shutterstock; Sergiy Kuzmin/Shutterstock; Ociacia/Shutterstock; HomeStudio/Shutterstock; Chiyacat/Shutterstock; archideaphoto/Shutterstock; pics five/Shutterstock; IB Photography/Shutterstock; sunsetman/Shutterstock; Jojje/Shutterstock; Lim Yong Hian/Shutterstock; Craig Jewell/Shutterstock; S-F/Shutterstock; Tetra Images/SuperStock; Stockbroker/MBI/Alamy; AsiaPix/SuperStock; **U3:** Hemis/Alamy; Ariel Skelley/Tetra Images, LLC/Alamy; Classic Collection/Shotshop GmbH/Alamy; Monkey Business Images/Shutterstock; Jolanta Wojcicka/Shutterstock; Ekkaruk Dongpuyow/Alamy; mamahoohooba/Alamy; Bill Miles/Cultura RM/Alamy; Keith Levit/Alamy; **U4:** Radius Images/Design Pics/Alamy; romakoma/Shutterstock; RDFlemming/Shutterstock; Khoroshunova Olga/Shutterstock; Andrew Holt/Alamy; Classic Collection/Shotshop GmbH/Alamy; Breadmaker/Shutterstock; Aardvark/Alamy; Westend61/Westend61 GmbH/Alamy; Flashon Studio/Shutterstock; Stockbroker/MBI/Alamy; Richard Newton/Alamy; **U5:** Frans Lemmens/Corbis; Pavel L Photo and Video/Shutterstock; Gelpi/Shutterstock; Fisher Litwin/Tetra Images/Alamy; Federico Rostagno/Shutterstock; Ilya Andriyanov/Shutterstock; Evgeny Bakharev/Shutterstock; miradrozdowski/YAY Media AS/Alamy; Valentina_G/Shutterstock; sbarabu/Shutterstock; foodfolio/foodfolio/Alamy; Liunian/shutterstock; **U6:** Christian Mueller/Shutterstock; Serg Salivon/Shutterstock; Sea Wave/Shutterstock; ThomsonD/Shutterstock; Chursina Viktoriia/Shutterstock; Sergio33/Shutterstock; Tarasyuk Igor/Shutterstock; Anna Kucherova/Shutterstock; Gino Santa Maria/Shutterstock; Viktor1/Shutterstock; V.S.Anandhakrishna/Shutterstock; Christopher Elwell/Shutterstock; Nattika/Shutterstock; Betacam SP/Shutterstock; Kitch Bain/Shutterstock; Garsya/Shutterstock; aarrows/Shutterstock; R. Fassbind/Shutterstock; colognephotos/Shutterstock; Denis Pogostin/Shutterstock; pattyphotoart/Shutterstock; l i g h t p o e t/Shutterstock; lunamarina/Shutterstock; Zoe Mack/Alamy; Julian Rovagnati/Shutterstock; Anna Moskvina/Shutterstock; ffolas/Shutterstock; PeJo/Shutterstock; xavier gallego morell/Shutterstock; Christian Draghici/Shutterstock; Da-ga/Shutterstock; janinajaak/Shutterstock; andersphoto/Shutterstock; Good Shop Background/Shutterstock; Vaclav Hroch/Shutterstock; Valentyn Volkov/Shutterstock; **U7:** Juniors Bildarchiv/F314/Juniors Bildarchiv GmbH/Alamy; irin-k/Shutterstock; pics five/Shutterstock; Luminis/Shutterstock; Phovoir/Shutterstock; Pressmaster/Shutterstock; Len44ik/Shutterstock; Monkey Business Images/Shutterstock; R-O-MA/ Shutterstock; silavsale/Shutterstock; Villiers Steyn/Shutterstock; **U8:** Villiers Steyn/Shutterstock; Don Mammoser/Shutterstock; Maurizio Photo/Shutterstock; Volodymyr Burdiak/Shutterstock; Matt Ragen/Shutterstock; Heiko Kiera/Shutterstock; Jolanta Wojcicka/Shutterstock; Erica Shires/Corbis; Joe McDonald/Corbis; Michael Potter11/Shutterstock; Purcell Pictures, Inc./Alamy; Petra Wegner/Alamy; Solvin Zankl/Nature Picture Library/Corbis; Juniors Bildarchiv BmbH/Alamy; LeonP/Shutterstock.

Front Cover Photography by Dimitri Otis/Stone/Getty Images.

Illustrations

Aphik; Bill Bolton; Chris Jevons (Bright Agency); Joelle Dreidemy (Bright Agency); Kirsten Collier (Bright Agency); Marcus Cutler (Sylvie Poggio); Marek Jagucki; Mark Duffin; Richard Watson (Bright Agency); Woody Fox (Bright Agency).